W9-CKJ-913

BEARING WITNESS

GENOCIDE AND ETHNIC CLEANSING IN THE MODERN WORLD™

THE
BOSNIAN WAR
AND ETHNIC CLEANSING

ZOE LOWERY AND JACQUELINE CHING

ROSEN
PUBLISHING

NEW YORK

Published in 2017 by The Rosen Publishing Group, Inc.
29 East 21st Street, New York, NY 10010

Library of Congress Cataloging-in-Publication Data
Names: Lowery, Zoe, author. | Ching, Jacqueline, author.
Title: The Bosnian War and ethnic cleansing / Zoe Lowery and Jacqueline Ching.
Description: New York : Rosen Publishing, 2017. | Series: Bearing witness:
  genocide and ethnic cleansing in the modern world | Includes
  bibliographical references and index. | Audience: Grade 7 to 12.
Identifiers: LCCN 2015049757 | ISBN 9781499463040 (library bound)
Subjects: LCSH: Yugoslav War, 1991–1995—Bosnia and Herzegovina. | Yugoslav
  War, 1991–1995—Atrocities—Bosnia and Herzegovina. | Yugoslavia—Ethnic
  relations.
Classification: LCC DR1313.3 .L68 2016 | DDC 949.703—dc23
LC record available at http://lccn.loc.gov/2015049757

Manufactured in China

CONTENTS

INTRODUCTION

History is full of stories of humankind engaging in all kinds of violence and killing, including wars, slayings, slaughters, and exterminations. It wasn't until the twentieth century, however, that a specific word and theory was created after World War II's gruesome executions of the Jewish people and other minorities: "genocide."

After seeing the horrors and annihilation of Assyrians in Iraq in 1933, Raphael Lemkin (1900–1959) coined the term "genocide." His definition included acts of barbarism that should be considered illegal at all times, even during wars. It's difficult to specify which acts are to be considered barbarous during war. It isn't as simple as counting the number of people killed. During the rule of England's King Henry VIII, seventy-two thousand executions took place. Europe's witch hunts (1450–1700) took forty thousand lives. As the Europeans settled in the Americas (1500s–1900), more than fifteen million Native Americans lost their lives. The African slave trade (1600s–1900s) was responsible for around sixty million African lives. And under the rule of China's Mao Tse-tung, about seventy million people were killed. Not one of these barbarous acts is usually defined as genocide.

Going beyond the definition of genocide as limited to mass killings, Lemkin characterized it as "a coordinated plan" to abolish the "essential foundations of the life of national groups, with the aim of annihilating the groups themselves." This more expansive definition of genocide refers the killing of a group of people, including the places where they lived, worshipped, and worked, in addition to their personal liberty, well-being, and self-respect.

The combat during the Bosnian War (1992–1995) was brutal between the area's three main cultural groups: Serbs, Croats, and Muslims. From the war's onset, the Bosnian Serb army started raiding and burning Bosnian Muslims' residences. The Muslim citizens were gathered, after which they were assaulted, slaughtered, or imprisoned. Up to twenty-six thousand Muslim residents had been methodically massacred by the time the war came to an end.

Thousands of porcelain cups are filled with traditional Bosnian coffee in memory of those who died and will not be there to sip the hot brew.

Widespread murder like that which occurred in Bosnia and other areas on the Balkan Peninsula has come to be described as "ethnic cleansing." The expression was reminiscent of Adolf Hitler's Final Solution during World War II, when, with the power of the Nazi regime, he used terrorization and oppression to try and "cleanse" Germany of its Jewish population, as well as other minorities. This came to be known as the Holocaust.

The very word "genocide" is certainly extremely weighted, whether it is used to describe modern events or those from years past. Legally speaking, it conveys more disgrace and conviction than many other terms used to describe the atrocities of war. Those who survive mass murders often feel that the term "genocide" should refer to their experience, whereas those accused of committing the crime of genocide vehemently reject it. To this day, courts, governments, and historians all over the world carefully review various events to determine whether or not they should be deemed genocide. For example, in October 2007, a U.S. House of Representatives panel debated and ultimately approved a resolution to formally acknowledge the mass murder of Armenians by Ottoman Turks during World War I. Turkey, a U.S. ally, was furious over this decision, even though the events occurred almost one hundred years ago.

CHAPTER 1

A BALKAN COUNTRY

Between 1918 and 1991, Yugoslavia was a southeastern European country comprised of the following republics: Bosnia and Herzegovina, Serbia, Croatia, Slovenia, Macedonia, and Montenegro. (It wasn't officially named Yugoslavia until 1929, however.) During the Yugoslav Wars in the 1990s, Yugoslavia crumbled after a succession of conflicts. The Bosnian War was among them.

The Bosnian War took place in the republic of Bosnia and Herzegovina. Three main ethnic groups live there: Muslims, Serbs, and Croats. As a result, there are at least three very different ways of viewing the Bosnian War. A bold war hero to one group might be a repressive dictator to another. A single territory may be claimed by many different groups. Self-defense can appear to others as aggression, and vice versa. As a result, judging events during wartime can be very confusing. The aftermath of the Bosnian War is still unfolding, and it will be a long time before the final word is written.

FORMER YUGOSLAVIA

★ Ljubljana
SLOVENIA

★ Zagreb

CROATIA

BOSNIA AND HERZEGOVINA

Sarajevo ★

Belgrade ★

SERBIA

MONTENEGRO

Podgorica ★

Priština ★

KOSOVO

★ Skopje

MACEDONIA

The six republics of Yugoslavia—Serbia, Croatia, Bosnia and Herzegovina, Slovenia, Montenegro, and Macedonia—broke up after the Yugoslav Wars.

REPUBLICS DECLARE INDEPENDENCE

The six republics that made up Yugoslavia differed greatly from each other. Each became an independent country at great human cost.

Serbia was the largest and most powerful of the former Yugoslav republics. Its dominance was a constant source of concern and resentment among the other republics. In 1992, during the Yugoslav Wars, Serbia and Montenegro together formed the Federal Republic of Yugoslavia. They stayed together until 2006, when Montenegro declared its independence. Serbia followed suit later that year.

Croatia, second among the former Yugoslav republics in size and power, declared its independence in 1991. However, the Croatian war of independence wore on until 1995. The wealthiest of the former republics, Slovenia, and the poorest, Macedonia, also declared their independence in 1991. Slovenia fought a Ten-Day War (June 26–July 7), but Macedonia remained at peace during the Yugoslav Wars.

Bosnia and Herzegovina, also called Bosnia, was the most ethnically mixed of all the Yugoslav republics. In 1991, the population of Bosnia and Herzegovina stood at 4.5 million. In Bosnia, which is slightly smaller than the U.S. state of West Virginia, 44 percent of the population was Muslim, 31 percent was Serb, and 17 percent was Croat. There were also small communities of Romanies (often called Gypsies), Jews, and ethnic Albanians.

Towns in Bosnia were typically mixed communities. Bosnian Serbs, Bosnian Croats, and Bosnian Muslims were friends and neighbors. They even intermarried. In contrast, the different ethnic groups in neighboring Croatia lived in separate parts of the republic. Religion tended not to divide Bosnians. The republic's Muslims, in particular, were not especially strict in their religious views. The government of Bosnia was headed by a seven-member presidency that included Croats, Serbs, and Muslims. This ensured that all groups were represented in the government. Despite these safeguards, a series of global and national events plunged these Bosnian groups into a brutal war with one another.

COMMON ANCESTRY

The Balkan peoples share a common ancestry that goes back 1,500 years. Serbs, Croats, Slovenes, Macedonians, and Montenegrins are all South Slavs. They are descendents of the central European Slavs who spread south into the Balkans around the sixth century CE. This region is home to other nationalities, too, such as Albanians, Romanies, Jews, and Turks.

The South Slavs are alike in physical appearance, and they speak languages that are closely related to one another. The umbrella term for the dialects spoken in the former Yugoslavia is "Serbo-Croatian." In addition, Serbs write in Cyrillic letters, as Russians do, while Croats use the Latin alphabet. The issue on which South Slavs have differed most is religion.

Over the centuries, many different forces brought change to the Balkan populations. War and migration were constants, with foreign tribes invading and local peoples relocating in their wake. In ancient times, the Illyrians, Thracians, and Dacians lived in the Balkan Peninsula. In the centuries to follow, the region was ruled by the Western Roman Empire, and then by its successor, the Eastern Roman Empire. The religion of the Western Roman Empire was Roman Catholicism; the religion of the Eastern, or Byzantine, Empire was Eastern Orthodox Christianity. Serbs, Macedonians, and Montenegrins practiced Orthodox Christianity. Most Croats and Slovenes living in the western part of the peninsula practiced Roman Catholicism.

Modern Serbs and Croats trace their connection to Bosnia back to the Middle Ages. Croats formed a state that lasted from 925 to 1102 CE. At its peak, Croatia stretched from the Adriatic coast into Serbia and included most of Slovenia.

As the Byzantine Empire declined, Serbia and Bulgaria conquered its remaining territories in Europe. By the mid-fourteenth century, Serbia was the most powerful kingdom in the Balkans. It controlled territories that later became part or all of Albania, Bulgaria, Greece, Macedonia, Montenegro, and Bosnia.

The region that is now Bosnia and Herzegovina lies

Ajvatovica is an event named after the devoted Muslim Ajvaz Dede, who sought to bring progress to the troubled Bosnia-Herzegovina region.

between the historical Serbian and Croatian territories. Both ethnic Serbs to the east, and ethnic Croats to the north and west, point to history to support their territorial claims in the region. Each of these ethnic groups identifies itself on the basis of culture, religion, and a common history. When one group perceives a threat from the other, war has often been the result.

OTTOMAN OCCUPATION

Byzantine rule in the Balkans ended with the arrival of the Ottoman Turks, a Muslim people from central Asia. They invaded Serbia in 1389 and Bulgaria in 1393, later expanding their territory to include most of Slavonia, and other parts of Croatia and Bosnia. The Ottoman Empire, also known as the Turkish Empire, remained in control for the next five hundred years. Constantinople, the former capital of the Byzantine Empire, was renamed Istanbul. From the beginning of Ottoman rule, waves of Serbs, Croats, Albanians, and other peoples migrated across the Balkans, trying to escape oppression or fighting.

EPIC POETRY

The Battle of Kosovo in 1389 was a defining event for the Serbs. It was fought between a united group of Serbian lords and the Ottoman Empire. Although the Serbs were no match for the Ottomans, a small Serbian state survived that brought about a Serbian cultural rebirth.

Today, the Battle of Kosovo is celebrated as a national holiday in Serbia.

Serbian epic poetry recounts the story of how Prince Lazar, the leader of the Serb forces, was visited by an angel the night before the battle. The angel offered a choice between an earthly kingdom and a heavenly one. Lazar chose the heavenly kingdom and, therefore, had to die on the battlefield.

Modern-day Serbian leader Slobodan Milošević would recall the Battle of Kosovo in order to gain support for his nationalistic goals. In 1989, on the six hundredth anniversary of the Battle of Kosovo, he talked about how the Serbs were still "engaged in battles and are facing battles" and how these could not be won "without resolve, bravery, and sacrifice, without the noble qualities that were present here in Kosovo in the days past."

According to Eric Black in *Bosnia: Fractured Region*, during the Ottoman occupation, "Bosnia absorbed the flavor of Ottoman culture. Mosques and other Turkish-style structures marked the landscape. People bought and sold goods in Turkish-style bazaars, and children were educated in Islamic schools. Bosnia became the most visible symbol of Ottoman rule in the Balkans."

By the late seventeenth century, the Ottoman Empire began to decline. Many Ottoman rulers, called sultans, were more interested in luxury than conquest, and gradually, they lost control of the empire's outer provinces.

REBELLION

By the beginning of the nineteenth century, systems of government were changing around the globe. Revolutions in America (1775–1783) and France (1789–1799), especially, changed the world and how ordinary people saw it. The American and French people were guided by principles of liberty and democracy. They rejected the old system in which a king was the absolute ruler. Instead, they wanted a society based on individual rights, freedom of religion, freedom of the press, and the rule of law. Around the world, people forged nationalist movements to bring about change. Above all else, these movements stressed the importance of a people's common culture, ethnic identity, and national origin.

SLAUGHTER OF THE KNEZES

The Janissaries, once an elite group of soldiers in the Ottoman army, had degenerated into outlaws at the end of the eighteenth century. They plundered and terrorized Serbian and Muslim villages in the Belgrade *pashalik*, or province. To prevent a Serbian revolt, the Janissaries began to decapitate the conspirators. Up to 150 prominent Serbs were killed. This mass murder is known as the Slaughter of the Knezes (local lords). Rather than stanch a revolt, the Janissaries' cruelty was the immediate cause of the Serbian uprising in 1804.

Serbs, for example, banded together and rebelled against the Ottoman rulers in 1804 and 1815, with Serbia becoming a semi-independent state. Greece, another Balkan nation, declared independence from the Ottoman Empire in 1829, and other states were to follow. In 1882, Serbia became the independent Kingdom of Serbia. This lasted until 1918, when it became part of Yugoslavia.

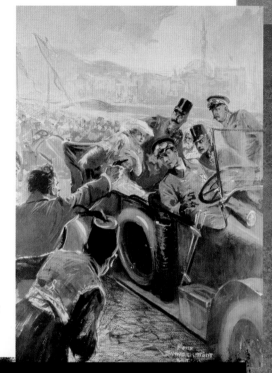

This image shows the assassination of Archduke Franz Ferdinand by Serbian nationalist Gavrilo Princip, an event that triggered World War I.

SEEKING A UNITED SOUTH SLAV STATE

Unlike Serbia, Bosnia was ruled by the Hapsburgs, an Austrian family, and was annexed by Austria-Hungary. Nationalism continued to rise among many groups in the Balkans, with the Ottoman Turks being driven out of Macedonia, most of Albania, and Kosovo during the First Balkan War of 1912–1913. The Second Balkan War, in 1913, was a territorial dispute between former Balkan allies.

A significant outcome of the Balkan Wars was that Serbia doubled in size and became a regional power. For the first time, Serbia appeared to have the military might to bring all the South Slav lands together. The leaders of Austria-Hungary saw this as a threat and looked for an excuse to wipe out Serbia. On June 28, 1914, they found their excuse: Serbian nationalist Gavrilo Princip assassinated Archduke Franz Ferdinand, heir to the Hapsburg throne. This event triggered World War I. Austria-Hungary accused Serbia of plotting the assassination and, a month later, declared war. Russia, along with France and Great Britain, backed Serbia. Germany, Bulgaria, and Turkey supported Austria-Hungary. By 1918, the end of World War I, millions had died and Europe was unrecognizable. The Ottoman and Austro-Hungarian empires had collapsed. Serbia had lost a quarter of its population, but at least it had come closer to the dream of a united South Slav state.

The Russian Empire also collapsed. It was replaced by a communist state called the Soviet Union. Its form of government, communism, aimed to establish a society without class divisions, in which property is owned not by individuals but by the community. This political system and philosophy was to be a major force in the world, including in the Balkans.

On July 28, 1919, the international community recognized a new Kingdom of Serbs, Croats, and Slovenes. It was renamed the Kingdom of Yugoslavia ("Land of the South Slavs") in 1929. Serbia was joined by Slovenia, Croatia, Bosnia and Herzegovina, Montenegro, and Vojvodina, a province that had been part of Hungary and had a large Serbian population. Yugoslavia's capital was Belgrade, the former Serbian capital, located in the north-central part of Serbia. Yugoslavia was ruled first by King Peter of Serbia and after his death by his son, Prince Aleksander.

Its parliament was dominated by Serbs.

The dream of South Slav unity had been realized. But from the start, there were demands for independence by non-Serbs, who resented Serbia's dominance in the new kingdom.

INVADED AND DIVIDED

Yugoslavia was torn apart again in World War II (1939–1945), which pitted the Allies against the Axis powers. At the outset of the war, Great Britain and France led the Allies. The Central Powers were Nazi Germany, Italy, and Japan.

In April 1941, Adolf Hitler invaded Yugoslavia and divided it up between Germany, Italy, Bulgaria, and Hungary. In Croatia, the Nazis installed a puppet government led by the Ustashe, a Croatian nationalist group. This so-called Independent State of Croatia included Bosnia and Herzegovina. In Nazi-occupied Serbia, the military and the police were in control.

The Ustashe ("rebels") had operated in Croatia before World War II. Under the Nazis, however, they began an immediate policy to rid the region of its Serbian Orthodox population. Its motto was: "One-third converted (to Catholicism), one-third expelled, one-third exterminated." Religion, especially, was used to distinguish the enemy. As far as the Ustashe was concerned, Eastern Orthodox Christians fell into the same category as Muslims. Both were non-Catholics and, therefore, had to be exterminated.

Under the Ustashe, tens of thousands of Serbs were sent to concentration camps. The largest of these was Jasenovac, known for the extreme cruelty with which its victims were tortured and killed. An estimated 330,000 to 390,000 Serbs were killed by the Ustashe.

Guerilla fighters organized a resistance against the Axis occupiers and the Ustashe. They were the Chetniks and the Partisans. The Chetniks wanted to restore the prewar Serbian monarchy. The Partisans were Serbs and non-Serbs who followed the communist leader Josip Broz Tito—an important figure in the second half of the century.

The puppet regime in Serbia began attacking Slavic Muslims, Serbian Jews, and Chetniks. These groups were sent to concentration camps near Belgrade, where nearly 90 percent of the Serbian Jewish population was killed.

The Allies decided to support Tito's Partisans, after their eight hundred thousand-strong army stood up to intense Axis attacks in 1943. In 1945, the Partisans won the war with the help of the Soviet Union. This left Tito in a position to dominate postwar politics and bring the communists to power.

World War II claimed the lives of 1.7 million Yugoslavs, many of whom were killed by other Yugoslavs. In addition, the country's major

Josip Broz Tito (*far right*) poses for a photograph with his staff at a hidden retreat in the mountains.

cities, industries, and communication systems were destroyed. Yugoslavia was left in such chaos that no one in the country or abroad believed it could be put back together. Yet Tito did.

A PERIOD OF PEACE

Beyond ridding Yugoslavia of the Ustashe and the Nazis, Josip Broz Tito had a vision for his country. His goal as leader of the Yugoslav Communist Party was to create a state based on the model of the Soviet Union. After the war, Tito was seen as a hero, not only by the Yugoslavs but also by the Allies, who put pressure on the last king of Yugoslavia to appoint him as premier.

Tito, who was half-Croat and half-Slovene, was in a position to chart the course for Yugoslavia. The Communist Party became the dominant party in Yugoslavia. Tito did away with the monarchy and divided the country into six republics and two provinces. In Tito's Yugoslavia, ethnicity was set aside in favor of what was good for the entire country. He made the expression of ethnic aspirations a serious crime. At the same time, he encouraged a broader national identity. When responding to a census, people increasingly identified themselves as "Yugoslav," instead of a particular ethnicity. In the decades after World War II, one-fourth of all marriages were mixed, involving people of different nationalities. For a while, it almost seemed as though the grudges of the past had been forgotten.

Tito was never interested in the welfare of Bosnian Muslims in particular, but he wanted to put an end to Serb and

Croat disputes over Bosnia. So, he gave Bosnian Muslims status as a nationality equal to that of the Croats, Serbs, Slovenes, and Macedonians. As a result, no group was more loyal than Bosnian Muslims to the concept of Yugoslavia.

Yugoslavia became the most open and prosperous Communist nation. Tito refused to follow orders from the Soviet Union, unlike the other Communist countries in Eastern Europe. Later, during the Cold War, he followed a policy of nonalignment. This gained him great support in the West.

Nevertheless, tensions boiled under the surface. The old nationalist complaints were heard once more. Serb nationalists wanted the power that they had had before the war. Croatia and Slovenia protested that their wealth was being used to prop up the poorer republics of Yugoslavia. Croatian leaders demanded more control over Croatian affairs.

Tito responded firmly to organized protests with mass arrests of protesters. But he also appeased them. In 1974, for instance, he created a constitution that established a new system of government giving more power to the six republics and to Kosovo and Vojvodina, which gained the right to self-rule.

This new system could not survive Tito's death in 1980. Ten years later, the country would descend into the most violent European conflict since World War II.

CHAPTER 2

PLUNGING TOWARD WAR

T he central government of Yugoslavia became shaky after Josip Broz Tito died in 1980. The lack of a strong national leader resulted in increased conflicts between ethnicities, and the separate republics became interested in their own securities and government power for themselves. Ambitious nationalist political leaders found a perfect storm of opportunity when an economic disaster during the 1980s collided with the Cold War's 1989 end.

One such leader, Slobodan Milošević, rose to power in Serbia. Historians largely blame him for the start of the Bosnian War. At a

Slobodan Milošević, shown here in 1999, rose to power in Serbia and is ultimately blamed for triggering the Bosnian War.

time when Serbs were suffering from economic problems, he stirred their nationalist feelings to promote his goal of forming a greater Serbia. Milošević rose to power in the Serbian government by making Kosovo a hotbed issue. Kosovo was one of the two Serbian provinces that had gained self-rule in 1974. In Kosovo, tensions between Serbs and an Albanian majority were escalating. (Albania borders Kosovo to the west.) When Milošević became Serbia's president in 1988, he passed amendments to the Serbian constitution giving his republic power over Kosovo and Vojvodina.

In Croatia and the other republics, the perceived threat of Serbian dominance seemed to be coming true. Croatia's first president, Franjo Tudjman, stoked the flames of Croatian nationalism. Although they were adversaries during the Croatian War (1991–1995), Milošević and Tudjman met several times in 1991 to discuss how Bosnia was to be divided between Croatia and Serbia. Once the Bosnian War began, Tudjman made his ambitions clear. In July 1992, with his unspoken approval, Croatian nationalists in Bosnia proclaimed an independent Republic of Herzeg-Bosnia within Bosnia and Herzegovina. These Croatians told the Bosnian Muslims within the new Republic of Herzeg-Bosnia to be grateful to them for "liberating" them from the Serbs. Tudjman pretended to have no part in it, but he was later found to have been the mastermind behind the independent Republic of Herzeg-Bosnia. The international community never recognized Herzeg-Bosnia, and in 1994 the highest court in Bosnia declared the young republic illegal.

Croatian president Franjo Tudjman looks on as Bosnian president Alija Izetbegović (*left*) shakes hands with Milošević in 1995 at the Dayton Peace Accords.

PROPAGANDA'S INFLUENCE

At the beginning of the Bosnian War, leaders like Slobodan Milošević and Franjo Tudjman used media outlets to rouse nationalist feelings among their countrymen. For instance, Serb radio and television concentrated on the atrocities (horrible acts) of the Ustashe against the Serbs during World War II. Such tactics brought Milošević and Tudjman broad support for their plans to go to war.

23

THE YUGOSLAV WARS

The Yugoslav Wars, which took place between 1991 and 2001, were fought largely between Serbs, on one side, and Croats and Muslims, on the other side. But it was also fought between Muslims and Croats within Bosnia, and between Macedonians and ethnic Albanians in Macedonia. These were the bloodiest conflicts on European soil since World War II.

In 1990, Communist regimes had fallen throughout Europe. The people of Poland, East Germany, Czechoslovakia, Bulgaria, Romania, and Hungary ousted their repressive Communist governments. In Yugoslavia, the ruling Communist Party also broke up, scattering power among the republics.

In June 1991, both Croatia and Slovenia declared their independence. In an effort to retain Slovenia, Yugoslavia fought the breakaway republic in the Ten-Day War, which ended with relatively few casualties. Slovenia's independence gained international recognition the following year. When Croatia declared its independence, however, it got a very different reaction from the central Yugoslav government. Slobodan Milošević, a Serb, invaded Croatia to "protect" Croatian Serbs. The latter, opposed to Croatian independence, created a Serbian state within Croatia, the Republic of Serbian Krajina.

The well-armed Yugoslav National Army, or JNA, then consisted mainly of Serb and Montenegrin soldiers. They inflicted huge casualties on the Croatian fighters, who were not an organized army but a group of lightly armed civilians. The worst part of the war was fought between 1991 and 1992, when

Serbs carried out mass executions. Fighting continued on a smaller scale until 1995, when a peace treaty was negotiated in Dayton, Ohio, between Tudjman, Milošević, and Bosnian president Alija Izetbegović.

TRIGGERING THE BOSNIAN WAR

While the fighting in Croatia continued, nearby Bosnia also began to experience internal unrest. Bosnian Croats and Muslims did not want to remain in a Yugoslavia dominated by Serbs. Such a situation would put them at the mercy of Milošević's oppressive rule. Macedonia had declared its independence at the end of 1991. If Bosnia were to follow the same course, it would likely be plunged into a war that was bloodier than the Croatian War. Therefore, Bosnian president Izetbegović appealed to Europe and the United States for help in avoiding bloodshed. He asked the United Nations (UN) to station troops in Bosnia. Not sensing the urgency of the situation, the UN sent just one hundred peacekeepers to monitor the situation. The UN also placed an arms embargo on Yugoslavia, hoping to limit any violence that might break out. The embargo, however, affected the warring sides unequally. It served to weaken the Bosnian army, which at that time was made up of mostly Muslims, as well as some Croats and even a few Serbs who chose to defend the legal government. The Bosnian Serb Army, on the other hand, was secretly being fed arms by Serbia.

Bosnian Serbs, who generally wanted to remain part of Yugoslavia, declared certain areas of northern and eastern Bosnia to be Serbian

Autonomous Regions. They threatened that if Bosnia voted to leave Yugoslavia, the Serbian Autonomous Regions would split from Bosnia and join up with Serb-dominated Yugoslavia. In March 1992, Bosnians held a referendum on independence. Nearly all Bosnian Serbs boycotted the vote, but of the Bosnians who did vote, more than 90 percent wanted independence from Yugoslavia. In response, the Bosnian Serbs declared their own independent state, Republika Srpska, formed out of the Serbian Autonomous Regions. Serbs soon began attacking the largely defenseless Bosnians.

On April 6, 1992, the European Community and the United States recognized Bosnia's independence, hoping that this would stabilize the republic. But on that day, Bosnian Serb paramilitary troops fired on a crowd of peace demonstrators in the Bosnian capital of Sarajevo. The Bosnian War had begun.

Only Serbia and Montenegro remained part of Yugoslavia. Milošević and his supporters argued that it was illegal for the other republics to declare independence from Yugoslavia. In this way, they justified a military assault on Bosnia. Under Serbian leadership, the JNA took control of 70 percent of the country in a matter of months. In addition, the JNA was ordered to blockade Sarajevo, one of the last major cities to hold out against Serbian forces. This job was left to Ratko Mladić, an army general and trusted henchman of Milošević. With the blockade in place, there was no way to get food or medical supplies into or out of the city. Water and electricity were shut off.

Believing that the war would last only a few weeks, the people of Sarajevo chose not to flee the city. In fact, it was the beginning of the four-year siege of Sarajevo, the longest siege in the history of modern warfare. The city had once been filled with fashionable cafés and nightclubs, and it even hosted the 1984 Winter Olympics. Now, it was constantly besieged with Serbian shells and sniper fire from fortified positions in the surrounding hills.

Seeing that Serbian aggression seemed unstoppable, the Croatian government entered the conflict. The first stop for the Croatian army was western Bosnia, where much of Bosnia's Croatian population lived.

ERASING ALL TRACES

The main obstacle that stood in the way of a Bosnian Serbian state was that there were many non-Serbs living in the area that the Bosnian Serbs claimed. Therefore, the Bosnian Serb army adopted a solution they had already started in Serb-occupied parts of Croatia: the "ethnic cleansing" of non-Serbs.

All of the groups involved in the war committed atrocities, but the Serbs committed them on a larger scale. Many in the Bosnian Serb Army were army regulars fighting for the ideals of a greater Serbia. But there were also many undisciplined volunteers among their forces—men who were merely fighting for plunder. They captured towns and villages and began terrorizing Muslims (and even fellow Serbs), taking valuables from the homes they raided.

To erase all traces of a Muslim or Croat presence in Republika Srpska, the Bosnian Serb army immediately rounded up non-Serbs for execution. Victims were often tortured to death. Muslim civilians were persecuted and killed not only by the Serbian forces, but also by their former friends and neighbors. Serbs who stayed friendly with Muslim neighbors or tried to protect them were considered traitors, and they were dealt with harshly. The army destroyed Catholic churches, monasteries, mosques, Islamic shrines and schools, and other places of cultural importance.

If they weren't killed outright, non-Serb refugees were rounded up and taken to one of the many concentration camps, where detainees were beaten and half-starved. Omarska camp was among the more notorious camps. Some detainees there were burned on a pyre of burning tires; others were forced to load dead bodies onto trucks or to dig their own graves.

The Bosnian Serb army executed and tortured many non-Serbs, leaving their bodies in mass graves. Others were sent to concentration camps.

Non-Serb women and girls were not spared. During the war, as many as fifty thousand Muslim girls and women, aged nine to sixty, were raped by Serbian soldiers and volunteers. This made them unfit, according to Muslim belief, to be either wives or mothers.

IMAGES SHOCK THE WORLD

Radovan Karadžić was the Bosnian Serb political leader at the beginning of the Bosnian War. In August 1992, he was interviewed by British media. When questioned about the concentration camps, Karadžić denied that atrocities were being committed in them. To support his claims, he invited some journalists to visit the camps in question. British Independent Television News (ITN) sent two film crews, which captured images of emaciated prisoners behind wire fences at Omarska and Trnopolje. The world was shocked, and some compared the images to those of Jews in the Nazi camps during the Holocaust.

In 1996, an article in *Living Marxism* charged that the images had "fooled the world," that they were manipulated by editing and camera angles. ITN responded to the charges by successfully suing for libel in 2000. The images of prisoners at Omarska and Trnopolje are still a prickly issue for revisionists who want to change the way history remembers the Bosnian War.

It is important to note that in the summer of 1992, Catholic Bosnian Croats and Muslims separately operated concentration camps, too, where they tortured and killed Bosnian Serb civilians. In establishing Herzeg-Bosnia, Croat extremists, led by Mate Boban, killed Muslims and other non-Catholics and marched them off to concentration camps. Once towns such as Mostar and Stolac were cleansed of non-Catholics, the Croat extremists also destroyed non-Catholic homes, places of worship, and monuments.

Most Bosnian Croats and Serbs had the option of fleeing to Croatia and Serbia. Bosnian Muslims, however, had nowhere

Muslim Croatians and Bosnians suffer without enough food in Manjaca, the largest Serbian concentration camp.

to go. They crowded into Bosnian cities that were still widely thought to be safe. When they arrived, however, Muslim refugees discovered that cities like Tuzla, Goražde, and Srebrenica were not safe at all. Serbian forces continued to carry out ethnic cleansing in these areas.

Some Muslims tried escaping into the western part of Bosnia but were repelled by the Croatian army, which occupied the region. This started fierce fighting between the Catholic Croats and Muslims. The Bosnian army swept through central Bosnia, destroying many Bosnian Croat villages in the process. In some cases, the Muslim-dominated Bosnian army used ethnic cleansing tactics similar to those employed by their enemies. In the town of Uzdol, for example, the Bosnian army killed dozens of Bosnian Croat civilians.

During the siege of Sarajevo, one act in particular struck a chord with the outside world. On February 6, 1994, Serbian forces shelled a crowded market in the city, killing nearly seventy civilians and wounding more than two hundred. Afterward, Serb snipers picked off civilian targets in the streets. After these attacks, outsiders were finally spurred to real action in order to protect defenseless civilians in Bosnia. Leaders of the North Atlantic Treaty Organization (NATO), a military alliance whose members include the United States and Canada, agreed on a military response. In its first use of force since its creation in 1949, NATO sent jets to shoot down Serbian aircraft over central Bosnia. Russia sent aid as well, contributing eight hundred peacekeepers to the UN forces already there.

CHAPTER 3

SEEKING SAFETY

Close to three-quarters of Bosnia was under Serb control by 1993. That May, the Bosnian cities of Sarajevo, Bihać, Goražde, Srebrenica, Tuzla, and Žepa were proclaimed to be official United Nations Security Council safe zones. UN peacekeeping troops would protect these areas using "all necessary means, including the use of force." Furthermore, the UN also demanded that Bosnian Serbs remove their militaries so that refugees could receive humanitarian assistance.

The term "safe area" was never properly defined. What made a city a "safe area"? Whose job was it to keep it safe? How much force was authorized to do so? When UN Secretary-General Boutros Boutros-Ghali requested 34,000 UN troops to safeguard the safe areas, no countries were willing to contribute troops. Finally, the UN Security Council authorized 7,300 troops. In fact, only 3,500 were deployed.

In the next two years, Bosnian Serbs continued to attack these supposedly safe cities. Troops blocked humanitarian aid and even detained some of the UN peacekeepers deployed there. The United Nations simply did not give the peacekeepers the firepower needed to protect the safe areas. In July 1995, Serbian forces defied the UN and suddenly attacked two safe areas, Srebrenica and Žepa.

SREBRENICA WATCH

Before the war, Srebrenica, a mining town in eastern Bosnia, had a population of ten thousand. Waves of refugees raised this number to sixty thousand. The Serbs badly wanted to capture Srebrenica because of its proximity to both the Republika Srpska and the border with Serbia.

The UN had declared the city a safe area, sending six hundred Dutch UN peacekeepers to guard it. But Srebrenica was under nearly continuous siege by Bosnian Serbs. In addition, the Bosnian army defending Srebrenica had run out of ammunition. Thousands of civilians, mostly Bosnian Muslims, were trapped in the city. The Serbs had banned supply convoys so many civilians were living on the streets, dying of cold and hunger and without medical supplies.

In July 1995, events in Srebrenica captured the world's attention. Over five days, the Bosnian Serb army murdered eight thousand Muslim boys and men. Earlier in March,

Republika Srpska president Radovan Karadžić ordered an offensive that would "create an unbearable situation."

the president of Republika Srpska, Radovan Karadžić, ordered the Bosnian Serb army to begin combat operations that would "create an unbearable situation . . . with no hope of survival or life for the inhabitants of Srebrenica." The Bosnian Serb offensive began on July 6, and by July 11, the city was captured.

The mass executions took place from July 12 to July 16, 1995. First, the men were taken to empty schools, soccer fields, or warehouses. Sometimes, they were detained for several hours before being loaded onto buses and driven to another site. Often blindfolded and with their hands tied behind their backs, they were lined up and shot. Many tried to flee to the mountains, but they were hunted down and killed or captured. These scenes were repeated at a dozen places around Srebrenica.

STUCK IN THE SREBRENICA STRUGGLE

Seventeen-year-old Emir Suljagić was living in Srebrenica when the UN peacekeepers arrived. Conditions in the UN safe area were terrible, with the Serbs continuously shelling the city and people living on the streets. Suljagić's father was killed by a Serb shell.

Suljagić thought the Dutch UN troops were inappropriately friendly with the Serbian soldiers. Nevertheless, he believed the UN would protect the people of Srebrenica. He was wrong. The safe area fell to the murderous Bosnian Serb Army. Among those killed was his seventy-year-old grandfather. Suljagić was one of the lucky ones who survived.

International War Crimes Tribunal workers uncover the bodies of victims from a mass grave in **1996**. Investigations like this discovered some of the horrible acts that occurred during the war.

After the war, several organizations worked to piece together what happened during the massacre in Srebrenica. Among them were the International Commission on Missing Persons and the International Criminal Tribunal for the Former Yugoslavia. Their researchers discovered that Bosnian Serb soldiers in Kravica threw grenades and opened fire on a warehouse where around two hundred men were being held. Victims of all ages, from eight to eighty-five years old, were found at a grave at Kozluk. Near Konjević Polje, the victims included women and younger children. Near the village

of Meces, Serb soldiers announced on megaphones that if the men surrendered, they would be safe. When the men did give up, about 150 of them were shot to death, but only after being forced to dig their own graves. Another group of about 260 men was ordered to stand still around a large pit. At the slightest motion, individuals were shot. In the end, the rest were pushed into the pit and buried alive.

Dutch UN peacekeepers were criticized for standing by while the Srebrenica atrocities took place. However, the area was too large for a force of four hundred lightly armed men to defend. (Their numbers had declined by this time.) In addition, the Dutch commander Colonel Karremans's repeated requests for air support and arms supplies were denied or ignored.

Commander Colonel Thomas J. P. Karremans repeatedly requested air support from NATO, but his requests were at first ignored.

In the mountains around Srebrenica, the killing continued for weeks. The Srebrenica massacre was the largest mass murder in Europe since World War II. Of all the massacres that took place during the Bosnian War, Srebrenica was the only one ruled by the International Court of Justice to be genocide.

CHAPTER 4

GLOBAL ACTION

Bosnian Muslim casualties from the Bosnian War reached more than twenty-six thousand. Those who starved to death or died before they could receive medical care numbered in the thousands. To this day, tens of thousands of Bosnian Muslim women were raped, and up to ten thousand Muslim citizens are missing. More than 2.2 million were relocated. Western media highlighted other governments' sluggish response to this bloodshed. Europe, the United States, and the United Nations all faced criticism for their failure to act early enough to prevent the genocide.

In the course of the war, the UN Security Council imposed economic sanctions, deployed peacekeepers, and helped deliver humanitarian aid. However, the countries that made up the Security Council were not motivated to use armed force. The United States is a particularly influential voice on the UN Security Council, but America was curiously silent when it came to events in Bosnia. "The United Nations can only be effective," said Richard Falk, a Princeton University professor, "when the U.S. and its close allies perceive a strategic interest at stake." Ultimately, Bosnia's tragedy did not pose an immediate threat to U.S. national interests.

There are questions about how much Western governments knew in the early days of the Bosnian War. The administration of U.S. president George H. W. Bush had heard stories about Omarska, but the conclusion was that these reports
were "unconfirmed." In the early 1990s, the Internet was still in

its infancy, and news
and images did not
circulate quickly from
the isolated regions
of Bosnia. However,
once Western jour-
nalists were given
access to the concen-
tration camps in
the summer of
1992, it became
harder to dismiss
knowledge of the
situation.

An Omarska torture camp survivor's
family member holds up a photograph
of the excavated bodies of the victims.

American diplomats and political leaders said the Bosnian War was a bitter civil conflict rooted in ancient hatreds.
The administration of George H. W. Bush admitted that the situation was a tragedy but claimed it was not a war of aggression
in which there were clear aggressors and victims. Nobody in
the highest government positions thought the war was worthy
of the potential high costs in terms of soldiers' lives and tax-
payers' dollars.

In addition, the American people were distracted for a

time by the humanitarian crisis unfolding in Somalia. President Bush chose to send twenty-eight thousand soldiers to feed the starving Somalis, rather than sending soldiers to Bosnia. After President Bill Clinton took office in 1992, economic sanctions and diplomatic pressure continued to be the tools used to address the violence in Bosnia. The United States' lack of decisive action even after Srebrenica was an embarrassment.

On August 28, 1995, when the Serbs shelled the Sarajevo market, the United States finally led a massive NATO bombing campaign. NATO planes carried out 750 attack missions in three weeks and sent the Serbs into retreat. By September 1995, the united forces of Croats and Muslims succeeded in cutting back Serbian control of 70 percent of Bosnia to just below 50 percent.

INTERNATIONAL CRIMINAL TRIBUNAL FOR THE FORMER YUGOSLAVIA (ICTY)

The United Nations wanted to bring those who committed war crimes in Bosnia to justice, so it created the International Criminal Tribunal for the Former Yugoslavia (ICTY) in 1993. In the beginning, only a few low-level war criminals were brought to trial. But in 1999, Slobodan Milošević became the first sitting president to be charged with war crimes. Milošević, the "Butcher of the Balkans," was charged with planning, organizing, and executing massacres in Bosnia and Kosovo. Milošević died in his cell on March 11, 2006, just a few months before his four-year-long trial was expected to conclude.

The ICTY, located in The Hague, the Netherlands, was the first international war crimes tribunal to be set up since the Nuremberg and Tokyo trials after World War II. International courts, represented by judges from around the world, step in when countries are unwilling or unable to bring their war criminals to justice. Sometimes, as in the case of Milošević, international courts are required because the criminals are still in power.

In part, the purpose of the ICTY was to give voice to the victims, who submitted their stories in testimony. ICTY lawyers and investigators also

Up To $5 Million Reward

Wanted

For crimes against humanity

Slobodan Milosevic
President of the Federal Republic of Yugoslavia

For genocide and crimes against humanity

Radovan Karadzic   Ratko Mladic

REWARDS FOR JUSTICE
Post Office Box 96781 • Washington, D.C. 20090-6781 U.S.A.
email: mail@dssrewards.net • www.dssrewards.net
1-800-437-6371 (U.S.A. Only)

Milosevic, Karadzic, Mladic have been indicted United Nations Interna Criminal Tribunal for the F Yugoslavia for crimes a humanity, including murde rapes of thousands of inn civilians, torture, hostage of peacekeepers, wa destruction of private pro and the destruction of places. Mladic and Kar also have been indicte genocide.

To bring Milosevic, Kar and Mladic to justice, the States Government is offe reward of up to $5 milli information leading to transfer to, or conviction Inter-national Criminal Tr for the Former Yugoslavia of these individuals or any person indicted by International Tribunal.

If you believe you information, please conta nearest U.S. embas consulate, or write the Department of State, Diplo Security Service at:

The U.S. State Department distributed wanted posters calling for information about Yugoslav president Slobodan Milošević, Radovan Karadžić, and Ratko Mladić.

made discoveries in the course of the trials about what really happened during the war. The ICTY wanted to avoid criticism that it was only looking to punish Serbs and Croats. Therefore, it has handed down indictments to a few senior Bosnian Muslim officers and Kosovar Albanians, too. In February 2007, the

ICTY made several rulings that failed to clarify Serbia's role and liability in the Bosnian War. First, the tribunal ruled that Serbia's campaign of ethnic cleansing against Bosnian Muslims did not constitute genocide. Only the massacre in Srebrenica met the court's requirements for genocide. In that case, however, the court ruled that Serbia could not be held accountable for the killing, as the orders to attack were not given by the Serbian government but by Radovan Karadžić, president of Republika Srpska. Serbia was reprimanded, however, for failing to intervene in the genocide.

The ICTY trials and appeals are expected to continue into 2017. The tribunal has indicted more than 160 individuals. When the trials eventually come to a close, there will still be many war crimes suspects to hold to account. At that point, the job of trying these individuals will have to be transferred to courts in individual countries. But in postwar Bosnia, where people are trying to rebuild their lives, there is doubt about whether going after war criminals is in the country's best interest. It might create even more tension, instead of helping people to heal and move on.

CHAPTER 5

HEALING

The war in Bosnia officially came to an end with the signing of the Dayton Peace Accords on December 14, 1995. President of Bosnia and Herzegovina Alija Izetbegović; Croatian president Franjo Tudjman; and Serbian president Slobodan Milošević all signed the peace agreement.

Some sixty thousand NATO troops were deployed in order to help Bosnia recover. They trained new army and police forces and escorted refugees back to their homes. Bos-nia is now divided into the Republika Srpska, domi-nated by the Serbs, and the Federation of Bosnia and Herzegovina, dominated by Bosniaks (Muslims) and Croats. Bosnia had been a mixed society before the war, with intermarriages, a common language, and

On December 14, 1995, the Dayton Peace Accords were signed, ending the war in Bosnia.

religious tolerance. Now, however, some villages within the country are completely populated by a single group.

There is reconstruction all over Bosnia today. Churches, mosques, roads, and bridges that were blown up are being rebuilt. There are other signs of progress. All Bosnians now share common passports, and they can travel freely and safely anywhere in the country. There is a common army, border police, customs, and defense ministry.

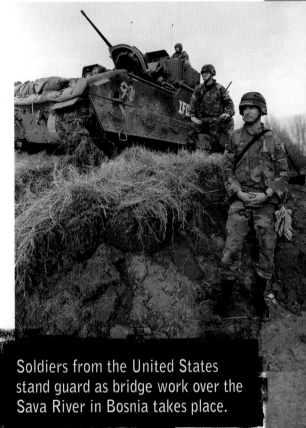

Soldiers from the United States stand guard as bridge work over the Sava River in Bosnia takes place.

Bosnia is currently working toward the goal of full membership in the European Union. But there are many obstacles. The administration of a country divided into three parts is costly and complex. Children attend segregated schools. In addition, the postwar government is weak, and efforts to strengthen central institutions have not worked so far. Some Bosnians prefer that the country be formally divided instead of the complicated government structure put in place by the peace agreement. Moreover, the economy is struggling, with very high unemployment and poverty.

According to the Bosnian constitution, the presidency is made up of a Bosniak and a Croat, elected from the Federation of Bosnia and Herzegovina, and a Serb, elected from the Republika Srpska. They serve a four-year term together.

In 2004, the sixty thousand NATO peacekeepers were replaced with seven thousand EU troops. In February 2007, the EU announced that it would cut these back to 2,500 by year's end. But Bosnia continues to be supervised by the Office of the High Representative of Bosnia. This international governor has the power to fire elected political leaders and impose laws. As of January 13, 2016, this office was held by Austrian diplomat Dr. Valentin Inzko.

POSTWAR BOSNIA

History books are often written about events that occurred in the distant past and about people who are long dead. The Bosnian War, on the other hand, took place so recently that questions of what really happened are still being debated. Even the

BRCKO

True to Balkan tradition, a single autonomous district exists in northeast Bosnia today: Brcko (pronounced birch-ko). It is the only multiethnic large city left in Bosnia, where Serbs, Croats, and Muslims work together and attend the same schools. The business climate there is stronger than in the rest of Bosnia, and the people have higher salaries.

war's official death toll is in doubt. Since 1994, the media has reported that a total of two hundred thousand people, civilian and military, were killed during the war. But in 2004, the ICTY cut that number in half, based on its research. Of the civilians killed, roughly 83 percent were Bosnian Muslims, 10 percent were Serbs, and 5 percent were Croats. In addition, smaller numbers of Jews, Romanies, and others are said to have died in the conflict. However, the research team concedes that their database is incomplete and the project is ongoing.

From the hunt for war crimes suspects to the search for missing persons, Bosnia continues to make headlines. In June 2007, Muslims from Srebrenica filed a civil action in the District Court of The Hague against the United Nations and the Dutch government for failing to protect the residents when the Serbs overran the city. It was filed on behalf of a group of survivors known as the Mothers of Srebrenica, who represent six thousand survivors of the massacre.

The District Court of the The Hague initially ruled that the United Nations was immune from prosecution. But on July 16, 2014, the court decided that the Dutch state was responsible for compensating relatives of the more than three hundred Muslim men who, on July 13, 1995, were deported from a Dutch compound and mostly killed by Bosnian Serbs.

International pressure was heavy on Serbia to hunt down and hand over fugitives to the ICTY. Serbia must cooperate with the tribunal in order to be considered for membership in the EU. The Serbian government initially offered a $1.4

INTERNATIONAL COMMISSION ON MISSING PERSONS

In 1996, the International Commission on Missing Persons (ICMP) was established to locate and identify missing persons from the wars in the former Yugoslavia. The ICMP identifies missing people by excavating graves and recovering human remains for DNA identification. As of 2015, according to Reuters reporter Daria Sito-Sucic, the organization had identified more than 70 percent of the thirty thousand remains that have been found. An estimated thirteen thousand individuals were still unaccounted for.

Former Bosnian Serb leader Ratko Mladić salutes the ICTY in 2011 after being declared fit to stand trial.

million reward for information leading to the capture of Ratko Mladić, the Bosnian Serb military leader. In October 2011, they increased their reward to about $13.9 million. This was in addition to the $5 million that the United States had already offered for information leading to the arrest of Mladić and Radovan Karadžić, both of whom had been accused of organizing the Srebrenica massacre. Mladić and Karadžić have both been captured and are standing trial in the International Criminal Tribunal for the Former Yugoslavia for war crimes. Judgments in their cases are expected in 2016 and 2017.

The tribunal for the former Yugoslavia as well as the International Court of Justice have both ruled that the atrocities meet the definition of genocide. However, a UN resolution that officially deemed the atrocities that occurred there a genocide did not pass. Russia vetoed the measure. China, Angola, Nigeria, and Venezuela abstained from voting. Serbia's president Tomislav Nikolic has made an apology for Srebrenica but has never gone so far as to refer to it as a genocide.

In July 2015, another 136 bodies were uncovered from mass graves. A family mourns over their loved one's coffin before it is buried.

Another continuing effort in Bosnia is the discovery and identification of bodies in the hundreds of mass graves found all over the country. In October 2007, a new discovery of a mass grave was made near Srebrenica. The remains of thirty-four Muslim civilians had been moved there from another grave in an attempt to cover up the killings. "Body parts from single victims have been found at multiple sites," writes *The Atlantic*'s David Rhode. "In one case, parts of the body of one victim were discovered in five mass graves." As of 2015, there have been ninety-three mass-grave exhumations and 6,827 DNA identifications of the dead.

What was left of Yugoslavia ended in 2006, when Montenegrins and Serbians declared their independence, thus becoming two separate countries, Montenegro and Serbia. In 2008, Kosovo declared its independence from Serbia. But the breakup of Yugoslavia and the wars that followed it will have consequences for years to come.

500–600 CE South Slavs move into the Balkans, probably from areas in modern-day Poland and Germany.

925–1102 CE The first united Croatian state is formed.

1346 The Kingdom of Serbia is established by King Stefan Dusan, becoming one of the larger states in Europe.

1389 On June 28, the Serbs are defeated by the Ottoman army at the Battle of Kosovo.

1463 Ottoman Turks conquer Bosnia and Herzegovina.

1882 Serbia is liberated from the Ottoman Empire, becoming once again the Kingdom of Serbia.

1908 Austria-Hungary annexes Bosnia and Herzegovina.

1912–1913 The Turks are driven out of most of the Balkan Peninsula in the First Balkan War. The Second Balkan War is fought in 1913 between the former Balkan allies.

1914 On June 28, Archduke Franz Ferdinand, heir to the throne of Austria-Hungary, is assassinated in Sarajevo by Gavrilo Princip, a Serb nationalist. This triggers World War I.

1918 World War I ends. Austria-Hungary collapses. Bosnia and Herzegovina becomes part of the new Kingdom of Serbs, Croats, and Slovenes.

1929 The Kingdom of Serbs, Croats, and Slovenes changes its name to the Kingdom of Yugoslavia.

1939 World War II begins with Germany's invasion of Poland.

1941 The Germans and Italians invade the Balkans. Bosnia and Herzegovina is annexed by the Nazi-supported Croatian Ustashe government. Thousands of Serbs, Jews, and Romanies are sent to concentration camps. A Nazi-run puppet government is established in Serbia.

1945 Bosnia is liberated by Communist Partisans led by Josip Broz Tito.

1946 Tito forms a Communist republic called the Federal People's Republic of Yugoslavia, composed of Bosnia and Herzegovina, Serbia, Croatia, Slovenia, Macedonia, and Montenegro.

1974 Tito creates a new constitution, giving decision-making power to the six republics and giving greater autonomy to the provinces Kosovo and Vojvodina.

1980 Tito dies. Without his tight rein, ethnic and nationalist tensions rise. A collective presidency rules until 1991.

1984 On February 8, the Winter Olympics opens in Sarajevo.

1991 The Soviet Union collapses. In June, Slovenia and Croatia each declare independence from Yugoslavia. Slovenia breaks away after the Ten-Day War. Croats and Serbs begin fighting in Croatia. In September, the UN imposes an arms embargo on Yugoslavia. In November, Bosnian Croats declare their own state, Herzeg-Bosnia.

1992 In January, Macedonia declares independence, followed by Bosnia on February 29. Bosnian Serbs declare a separate state (later called Republika Srpska). On April 5, Bosnian Serbs begin their siege of Sarajevo, which lasts until February 29, 1996. On April 6, war erupts in Bosnia. In

August, the world is shown shocking pictures of emaciated Muslims held in Bosnian Serb concentration camps.

1993 The UN declares six "safe areas" for Bosnian Muslims: Sarajevo, Tuzla, Bihać, Srebrenica, Žepa, and Goražde. Bosnian Croats and Muslims fight each other over the one-third of Bosnia not yet controlled by the Bosnian Serbs.

1994 Serbian forces shell a Sarajevo market, killing sixty-eight people.

1995 On July 11, Bosnian Serbs seize Srebrenica and murder eight thousand Muslim boys and men over five days. In November, Bosnian president Alija Izetbegović, Croatian president Franjo Tudjman, and Serbian Slobodan Milošević sign the Dayton Peace Accord to end the war in Bosnia.

1996 The International Criminal Tribunal for the Former Yugoslavia (ICTY) begins work in The Hague.

2001 Milošević is arrested by Yugoslavian authorities and in June is turned over to the ICTY.

2002 In February, the trial of Milošević begins on charges of war crimes and crimes against humanity in Bosnia, Croatia, and Kosovo and for committing genocide in Bosnia.

2006 Milošević dies of a heart attack in his cell in The Hague, the Netherlands, before the completion of his trial.

2008 Radovan Karadžić is arrested after evading authorities for twelve years.

2009 Karadžić's trial at ICTY begins.

2011 Ratko Mladić is arrested after sixteen years on the run.

2012 Mladić's ICTY trial on charges of war crimes begins.

GLOSSARY

Allies In World War II, the major Allied powers included Britain, France, the Soviet Union, and the United States

annex To take territory by conquest.

annihilation A total elimination.

autonomous Describing a region or area that is part of a country but has self-governing powers.

Axis In World War II, the major Axis powers included Germany, Italy, and Japan. They fought the Allied powers.

Cold War The period of conflict and rivalry between the United States and the Soviet Union along with their allies, from the mid-1940s to the early 1990s.

communism Political theory and movement that abolishes private ownership.

concentration camp A compound where prisoners of war are confined, usually under harsh conditions.

embargo A government order prohibiting trade to a particular place, usually to warn or punish a group.

ethnic cleansing Various practices aimed at ridding a territory of a particular ethnic group.

federation A form of government in which states or groups are governed by a central authority.

genocide Systematic killing of a racial or cultural group.

International Court of Justice (ICJ) The main

judicial body of the United Nations. It is based in The Hague, the Netherlands.

International Criminal Tribunal for the Former Yugoslavia (ICTY) A judicial body of the United Nations established in 1993 to prosecute serious crimes committed during the Yugoslav Wars.

nonalignment When a country is not a participant with other countries in a pact or a treaty.

North Atlantic Treaty Organization (NATO) The international organization created in 1949 by the North Atlantic Treaty for the collective security of its members.

referendum A popular vote that is held to give final approval of a legislative act to the voting public.

regime The governing authority.

reprimand To formally scold or censure.

Republic of Herzeg-Bosnia Entity located within Bosnia and Herzegovina between 1991 and 1994 created by Croatian extremists during the Bosnian War and never officially recognized.

Republika Srpska One of two entities comprising the country of Bosnia and Herzegovina. It was created by Bosnian Serbs in response to the declaration of Bosnia's independence from Yugoslavia in 1992.

tribunal An assembly, including one or two judges, to conduct the business of a court of justice.

FOR MORE INFORMATION

Bosnian Canadian Relief Association
122 North Queen Street
Toronto, ON M8Z 2E4
Canada
(416) 236-9411
Website: http://bosnianrelief.org
Formed in 1992, this organization was created to help with
the disaster in Bosnia and continues its efforts with humanitarian support for civilians in Bosnia and Herzegovina.

Canadian International Development Agency
Global Affairs Canada
200 Promenade du Portage
Gatineau, QC K1A 0G4
Canada
(819) 997-5006
Website: http://www.acdi-cida.gc.ca/index-e.htm
E-mail: info@acdi-cida.gc.ca
This Canadian government agency is committed to reducing
poverty, promoting human rights, and supporting sustain-
able development.

Center for Balkan Strategies
126 Strada Traian Vuia
Cluj-Napoca, Cluj County
Romania

Website: /contact-us.html

The Center for Balkan Strategies is a nonprofit organization dedicated to contributing "to the regional development of the South-Eastern Europe, with focus on the non-EU Balkan states."

Human Rights Watch
350 Fifth Avenue, 34th Floor
New York, NY 10118-3299
(212) 290-4700
Website: http://hrw.org
E-mail: hrwnyc@hrw.org

Human Rights Watch is an independent, nongovernmental agency that conducts fact-finding investigations into human rights abuses in all regions of the world. It called for an international war crimes tribunal for the former Yugoslavia.

North Atlantic Treaty Organization (NATO)
NATO Headquarters
Boulevard Leopold III
1110 Brussels, Belgium
Website: http://www.nato.int
E-mail: natodoc@hq.nato.int

NATO is an alliance of twenty-six countries from North America and Europe committed to safeguarding the freedom and security of its member countries by political and military means. It plays an important role in crisis management and peacekeeping.

United Nations Mission in Bosnia and Herzegovina
 (UNMIBH)
United Nations Headquarters
1st Avenue, United Nations Plaza
New York, NY 10017
(212) 963-4475
Website:http://www.un.org/en/peacekeeping/missions/past/
 unmibh
Set up in 1995, UNMIBH coordinated UN activities in Bosnia, such as humanitarian relief and refugees, removing
 mines, human rights, elections, and rehabilitation of infra-
 structure and economic reconstruction. It was concluded in
 December 2002.

WEBSITES

Because of the changing nature of Internet links, Rosen Publishing has developed an online list of websites related to the
subject of this book. This site is updated regularly. Please use
this link to access the list:
http://www.rosenlinks.com/BWGE/bosnia

Black, Eric. *Bosnia: Fractured Region*. Minneapolis, MN: Lerner Publishing Group, 1999.

Cothran, Helen, ed. *War-Torn Bosnia*. Farmington Hills, MI: Greenhaven Press, 2001.

Cruden, Alexander. *The Bosnian Conflict* (Perspectives on Modern World History). Farmington Hills, MI : Greenhaven Press/Gale, Cengage Learning, 2012.

Englar, Mary. *Bosnia-Herzegovina in Pictures*. Kent, England: Twenty-First Century Books, 2007.

Filipovic, Zlata. *Zlata's Diary: A Child's Life in Wartime Sarjevo*. Rev. ed. New York, NY: Penguin, 2014.

Fireside, Harvey, and Bryna J. Fireside. *Young People from Bosnia Talk About War*. Berkeley Heights, NJ: Enslow Publishers, 1996.

Friedman, Mark D. *Genocide* (Hot Topics). Chicago, IL: Heinemann Library, 2012.

King, David C. *Bosnia and Herzegovina*. New York, NY: Benchmark Books, 2005.

January, Brendan. *Genocide: Modern Crimes Against Humanity*. Minneapolis, MN: Twenty-First Century Books, 2007.

Perl, Lila. *Genocide*. New York, NY: Cavendish Square, 2011.

Sacco, Joe. *Safe Area Goražde. The War in Eastern Bosnia: 1992–95*. 10th ed. Seattle, WA : Fantagraphics Books, 2012.

Tekavec, Valerie. *Teenage Refugees from Bosnia-Herzegovina Speak Out*. New York, NY: Rosen Publishing Group, 1999.

BIBLIOGRAPHY

BBC.co.uk. "1995: Srebrenica—A Survivor's Story." Retrieved September 15, 2007 (http://news.bbc.co.uk/onthisday/hi /witness/july/11/newsid_4649000/4649933.stm).

Bilandzic, Dusan, et. al. *Croatia: Between War and Independence*. Zagreb, Croatia: The University of Zagreb and OKC Zagreb, 1991.

Bilefsky, Dan, and Somini Sengupta. "Srebrenica Massacre, After 20 Years, Still Casts a Long Shadow in Bosnia." *New York Times*, July 8, 2015. Retrieved December 15, 2015 (http://www.nytimes.com/2015/07/09/world/europe/sre-brenica-genocide-massacre.html?ref=topics).

Borger, Julian. "Radovan Karadžić, Europe's Most Wanted Man, Arrested for War Crimes." *The Guardian*, July 21, 2008. Retrieved December 15, 2015 (http://www.theguardian .com/world/2008/jul/22/warcrimes.internationalcrime).

Economist.com. "The Balkan Patient: A New International Governor Takes Over a Still Divided Country." June 28, 2007. Retrieved November 7, 2007 (http://www.economist. com/world/europe/displaystory.cfm?story_id=9409321).

Economist.com. "The Hinge in the Bracket: Bosnia's Only True Multi-Ethnic Place Sets an Example for the Country." June 28, 2007. Retrieved November 7, 2007 (http://www.economist .com/world/europe/displaystory.cfm?story_id=9409312).

Economist.com. "Peaceful, Rebuilt But Still Divided." November 24, 2005. Retrieved November 7, 2007 (http://www .economist.com/world/europe/displaystory.cfm?story _id=E1_VNNVVRP).

Economist.com. "Where the Past Is Another Country." March 1, 2007. Retrieved November 7, 2007 (http://www.economist .com/world/europe/displaystory.cfm?story_id=8786243).

Engelberg, Stephen. "Conflict in the Balkans; Weighing Strikes in Bosnia, U.S. Warns of Wider War." *New York Times*, April 25, 1993.

Falk, Richard A. Global Policy Forum. "1994 Conference on Security Council Reform." May 23, 1994. Retrieved September 28, 2007 (http://www.globalpolicy.org/security/conf94/falk.htm).

Genocid.org. "Bosnia Genocide." Retrieved October 12, 2007 (http://www.genocid.org/english.php).

Gerolymatos, Andre. *The Balkan Wars: Conquest, Revolution, and Retribution from the Ottoman Era to the Twentieth Century and Beyond*. New York, NY: Basic Books, 2002.

Gutman, Roy. *A Witness to Genocide: The 1993 Pulitzer Prize-Winning Dispatches on the 'Ethnic Cleansing' of Bosnia*. New York, NY: Macmillan Publishing Company, 1993.

Hanke, Steve H. "Inflation Nation." Cato Institute, May 26, 2006. Retrieved November 7, 2007 (http://www.cato .org/pub_display.php?pub_id=6406).

History World. "History of the Balkans." Retrieved October 4, 2007 (http://www.historyworld.net/wrldhis /PlainTextHistories.asp?historyid=ac79).

Hronesova, Jessie. "Bosnia: The Search for Missing Persons." Justice Info, May 28, 2015. Retrieved December 15, 2015 (http://www.justiceinfo.net/en/component/k2/316-bosnia -the-search-for-missing-persons.html).

ICRC Advisory Service on International Humanitarian Law. "The Prosecution v. Saric, Eastern Division of High Court (Third Chamber)." November 25, 1994. Retrieved November 7, 2007 (http://www.icrc.org/ihl-nat .nsf/39a82e2ca42b52974125673e00508144 /9d9d5f3c500edb73c1256b51003bbf44!OpenDocument).

International Commission on Missing Persons. Retrieved from October 2 to October 16, 2007 (http://www.ic-mp.org /home.php).

International Crimes Database "Mothers of Srebrenica et al v. State of The Netherlands and the United Nations." 2013. Retrieved December 15, 2015 (http://www .internationalcrimesdatabase.org/Case/769 /Mothers-of-Srebrenica-v-the-Netherlands-and-the-UN).

International Criminal Tribunal for the former Yugoslavia (ICTY). "Bosnia: Local Trials as Hague Tribunal Winds Down." February 12, 2007. Retrieved November 7, 2007 (http://hrw.org/english/docs/2007/02/12/bosher15296.htm).

International Criminal Tribunal for the former Yugoslavia (ICTY). "Prosecutor vs. Krstic, Appeals Chamber Judgment." United Nations, April 19, 2004.

Judah, Tim. *The Serbs: History, Myth and Destruction of Yugoslavia.* New Haven, CT: Yale University Press, 2000.

The Netherlands Institute for War Documentation (NIOD). "Srebrenica: Reconstruction, Background, Consequences, and Analyses of the Fall of a Safe Area." May 2003. Retrieved November 7, 2007 (http://publications.niod.knaw.nl /publications/srebrenicareportniod_en.pdf.

Riedlmayer, András J. "Destruction of Cultural Heritage in Bosnia-Herzegovina, 1992–1996: A Post-war Survey of Selected

Municipalities." Milošević Trial Public Archive.

Rohde, David. "A Cautionary Tale for U.S. Before It Enters Bosnia." *New York Times*, October 13, 1995.

Rohde, David. "Denying Genocide in the Face of Science." *The Atlantic*, July 17, 2015. Retrieved December 15, 2015 (http://www.theatlantic.com/international/archive/2015/07/srebrenica-massacre-bosnia-anniversary-denial/398846).

Sengupta, Somini. "Russia Vetoes U.N. Resolution Calling Srebrenica Massacre 'Crime of Genocide.'" *New York Times*, July 8, 2015. Retrieved December 15, 2015 (http://www.nytimes.com/2015/07/09/world/europe/russia-vetoes-un-resolution-calling-srebrenica-massacre-crime-of-genocide.html).

Sowards, Steven W. Twenty-Five Lectures on Balkan History. "Lecture 10: The Great Powers and the 'Eastern Question.'" Retrieved October 9, 2007 (http://staff.lib.msu.edu/sowards/balkan/lect10.htm).

Sudetic, Chuck. "Conflict in the Balkans; Bosnian Muslims Fleeing Villages Under Shellfire." *New York Times*, March 4, 1993.

Sudetic, Chuck. "As Formal End Nears, Some Lament Passing of the Yugoslavia They Knew." *New York Times*, January 15, 1992.

Sun-Sentinel.com. "Bosnia-Herzegovina: Mass Grave Yields Remains of Srebrenica Massacre." Retrieved October 12, 2007 (http://www.sun-sentinel.com/news/nationworld/sfl-fl12aworlddig10123nboct12,0,4175008.story).

Time.com. "Beyond Dictatorship." January 20, 1967. Retrieved November 7, 2007 (http://www.time.com/time/magazine/article/0,9171,843306,00.html).

Time.com. "Proletarian Proconsul." September 16, 1946. Retrieved November 7, 2007 (http://www.time.com/time /magazine/article/0,9171,888309,00.html).

Tran, Mark, Fred Attiwill, and agencies. "Turkish Ambassador Recalled from U.S. in Armenian Genocide Row." *Guardian Unlimited*. Retrieved October 13, 2007 (http://www.guardian .co.uk/turkey/story/0,,2188509,00.html).

U.S. Department of State. "U.S. Relations with Serbia." (http:// www.state.gov/r/pa/ei/bgn/5388.htm).

Wedgewood, Ruth. "Slobodan Milošević's Last Waltz." *New York Times*, March 12, 2007.

Wood, Nicholas. "Bosnia Plans to Expel Arabs Who Fought in Its War." *New York Times*, August 2, 2007.

Zimmerman, Warren. *Origins of a Catastrophe: Yugoslavia and Its Destroyers—America's Last Ambassador Tells What Happened and Why*. New York, NY: Times Books, 1996.

INDEX

ABOUT THE AUTHOR

Zoe Lowery is an avid student of history, constantly reading and studying about the past and other thought-provoking topics. She has written and edited a number of books on the topic for Rosen Publishing. Lowery lives in Colorado.

Jacqueline Ching is an author with a particular interest in writing about history. She has penned several books for Rosen Publishing, including *Women's Rights: Individual Freedom, Civic Responsibility*, and *The Assassination of Martin Luther King Jr.* Ching has also written for *Newsweek* and the *Seattle Times*. Today, she concentrates on writing for children and teens.

PHOTO CREDITS